Original title:
A Heart Full of Thanks

Copyright © 2024 Creative Arts Management OÜ
All rights reserved.

Author: Isaac Ravenscroft
ISBN HARDBACK: 978-9916-94-330-4
ISBN PAPERBACK: 978-9916-94-331-1

Heartstrings of Appreciation

When life hands you lemons, make some pie,
Or better yet, wear them as a tie.
Gratitude in every silly chore,
Just look at that lawn, it's less of a bore!

Thanks for the socks that never match,
And for your jokes that make me scratch.
You know, the ones that make me snort,
Like my cat in a sudden foot sport!

For all the meals burnt to a crisp,
I thank you for each tasty lisp.
Your culinary skills are quite the gem,
Like popcorn served without a stem!

So here's a toast, with some odd drinks,
To all the days spent giggling in sinks.
Laughter lingers in every dawn,
With quirky moments from dusk till the morn!

A Sanctuary of Thanks

In my castle of cushions, I nestle tight,
Thankful for moments that bring me delight.
Like cereal spills on a glossy floor,
Each crunch feels like laughter, what's not to adore?

To the dog that wags and steals my food,
You're the reason I'm always in a good mood.
Thank you for warming my cozy chair,
And your soft little snores that fill up the air!

For the friends who pop in for a snack,
And leave my fridge just slightly stacked.
With every slice of cake that we share,
I chuckle at frosting stuck in your hair!

To the quirks of life, I raise a cheer,
For all the moments that keep us near.
With laughter we blend, like spices in stew,
In this founded sanctuary, I'm grateful for you!

Emotions Woven in Appreciation

With smiles that stretch from ear to ear,
I thank the fridge for snacks so near.
The toast that pops, the tea that brews,
Each little joy is news I choose.

A sneeze of joy, a dance on toes,
For tiny things like socks that pose.
The cat's soft purr, the dog's wild chase,
In life's small moments, I find my grace.

The Thread of Gratitude

In the web of life, I find delight,
The coffee spills, oh what a sight!
The books I read, more plots than real,
Each misplaced pen is a laugh I feel.

The sun that shines on rainy days,
The way my hair gets crazy plays.
A missed bus ride, that time I tripped,
In funny fails, my heart is tipped.

Sunshine in Clouded Hearts

When skies turn gray, I wear my grin,
I'll dance in puddles, let the fun begin.
For every slip that draws a cheer,
I thank the world for this wild sphere.

Like sprinkles bright on chocolate cake,
A friend's loud laugh in silly flake.
The mishaps turn to joyful art,
As sunny rays fill up my heart.

Grateful for the Ordinary

A sock that's lost, a shoelace tied,
In all the mess, I'll laugh and glide.
The cereal spills—what a delight,
Each clumsy moment feels just right.

Thanks for the chair that creaks and groans,
The quirky way I sometimes moan.
For doors that swing when I should push,
In every blunder, life's a cush.

A Celebration of Simple Blessings

I tip my hat to the sunny skies,
For keeping me warm and free of flies.
To coffee most mornings, a magical brew,
Without you, morning meetings I'd rue.

A thank you to socks that stay in a pair,
And filled fridges that shimmer with contents to share.
To ice cream that melts on a hot summer day,
You're the key to making work just a ballet.

Radiant Echoes of Appreciation

To my cat, who thinks she's a queen on her throne,
She judges my snacks like a well-known loan.
To friends who make memes and spread endless cheer,
Without you, my phone would be far too austere.

I cherish the laughter that fills up the air,
And moments of dance with zero disguise.
For the quirks in my life, I raise up a cup,
Each smile's a treasure, just filling me up.

Seeds of Thankfulness

Here's to the couch, oh so comfy and wide,
Where I binge-watch my dramas, my beloved guide.
To leftovers hidden behind Tupperware,
A treasure to find, with flavors to spare.

I thank the good weather on weekends at last,
No rain upon plans, let's have a blast.
To jeans that still fit after all that I've snacked,
In this dance of my life, the joy is intact.

The Art of Recognizing Blessings

To the Wi-Fi that's strong through thick and thin,
You hold the remote to everyone's grin.
For instant replies that brighten my chat,
A quirky remark, or a silly meme rat.

Here's to the shoes that never feel tight,
That let me embrace my adventurous flight.
And moments of joy that often surprise,
With each little blessing, I realize, I rise.

Sowing Seeds of Appreciation

In the garden of my mind, I sow,
Wit and joy in rows that grow.
With every chuckle, with every cheer,
I plant my thanks, year after year.

Spilling coffee on my shoes today,
Is just another funny way to play.
Each blunder, a reminder, can you see?
Life's quirks are treasures for me!

Embracing the Present

Caught in this moment, oh what a treat,
Trying to dance with two left feet.
The slip, the stumble, I can't help but grin,
Thankful for the joy right from within.

My cat's on the keyboard, typing away,
Adding humor to this very day.
With every purr, a laugh does arise,
In the chaos, joy opens our eyes.

Cup Overflowing with Joy

My cup runneth over, spills on the floor,
Sometimes it's coffee, sometimes it's more!
The mess reminds me to take a break,
Thankful for laughter in every mistake.

I'm tripping on shoelaces like a clown,
Yet there's joy in falling, never a frown.
With giggles and snorts complimenting my fall,
Cheers to this life, funny moments for all!

The Melody of Grateful Hearts

In the symphony of laughter we share,
Each note strummed with a bit of flair.
Echoes of joy, they tickle the day,
I'm thankful for quirks that come out to play.

With a sock on my foot and a shoe on my head,
Every mix-up brings smiles instead.
Rhythm of chaos, a melody sweet,
In this dance of life, nothing's complete!

Brick by Brick

I built a wall, not with bricks,
But with all my grateful kicks.
Each laugh and smile, a solid stone,
Constructing joy, I claim my throne.

With every thanks, I raise a layer,
A silly dance, a goofy prayer.
Mortar made of jokes and glee,
My gratitude, as strong as me!

Built on Thanks

I built a castle in the sky,
With thankfulness that flips and flies.
Each floor a giggle, each room a pun,
A whimsical home where joy is spun.

The doors are laughter, windows bright,
My walls are hugs that feel just right.
A roof of chuckles, sunny beams,
This palace dreams in wacky themes.

Sailing on Waves of Appreciation

I sail a ship, the waves so high,
With gratitude and jelly pie.
The wind is laughter, sails so wide,
On waves of thanks, I take a ride.

Each splash a chuckle, every swell,
A funny tale I love to tell.
My anchor's joy, it holds me tight,
I navigate the sea of light.

Illuminating Shadows with Thanks

In shadows deep, I can be found,
With gratitude, I jump around.
I shine a light on silly fears,
And tickle gloom with funny cheers.

Thanks are lanterns, glowing bright,
Illuminating all that's light.
I dance 'neath stars, with joy I prance,
In shadows' corners, my heart's a dance.

A Bouquet of Grateful Thoughts

I gather blooms with laughter's scent,
A bouquet made, no money spent.
Each petal's pink with giggles sweet,
A floral joke you can't defeat.

I tie them up with joy and glee,
A gift for you from silly me.
In grateful gardens, see them grow,
A vibrant rainbow, full of show.

A Stone Path of Thanks

With every step upon this rock,
I trip and laugh, what a shock!
I dodge the weeds and lowly grass,
Grateful I'm not a bumbling ass.

The stones may shift, my ankle twist,
But I'm still here, so can't resist.
Each stumble's worth a giggle or two,
It's proof of life's grand view.

As I hop and skip along this way,
I'm thankful for each silly sway.
For laughter brightens even the fall,
A stone path's just life's funny call.

So I gather stones, like memories dear,
Every clumsy trip brings cheer.
With chuckles echoing, loud and clear,
I strut my gratitude without fear.

The River of Appreciation

Floating boats on water's gleam,
Each wave is thanks—it's a dream!
I paddle hard, but life's a splash,
Grinning wide—it's quite the bash!

The ducks quack loud, join in my glee,
They're paddling wits, it's quite the spree!
I toss a crumb, they flap and play,
"Thank you, ducks!" I laugh all day.

The current pulls, I swirl and swish,
I'm grateful for this quirky wish.
As I drift past all that's bright,
I grin at all this sheer delight.

Oh, river wide, you bring me cheer,
Life's little hiccups disappear.
With every splash, I sing and say,
Appreciation's in the play!

Wings of a Grateful Spirit

With flapping wings, I soar so high,
Even if I tumble from the sky.
Each feather catches breezes tight,
I laugh at clouds and greet the light.

I thank the trees for their embrace,
Even when I crash and lose my place.
A clumsy glide, a twirl, a twist,
Gratitude's humor is hard to resist.

Soaring birds, oh what a sight,
We chuckle as we chase the light.
In every dive and wayward spin,
The joy of thanks is where I've been.

With every flap and every glide,
I honor whims, nothing to hide.
For gratitude's flight is wild and free,
Flying high, just laugh with me!

Cherished Moments of Remembered Joy

From cookies baked with laughter loud,
To sneaky spills that draw a crowd.
Each mix-up, a treasured delight,
In the kitchen, chaos takes flight.

Dance floors echo with feigned grace,
I trip and twirl, it's a wild race.
Thankful for friends who join the scheme,
Together we burst out in gleeful scream.

Picnics turned into puddly games,
We've lost our shoes, but not our names.
Every giggle, every silly sigh,
Create a scrapbook that can't run dry.

So let's raise a glass, not to forget,
For every blunder, there's no regret.
In moments lived with joy so swift,
Laughter's the greatest gift!

Through the Lens of Gratitude

When coffee's hot and spills a bit,
I laugh it off, don't throw a fit.
For every drop that stains my shirt,
It's fuel for joy, and that's my perk.

The mailman waves, I wave back too,
His delivery skills? Quite askew!
But every package brings a smile,
And all it takes is just a while.

The cat jumps high, then lands in grace,
I chuckle as she makes her face.
For all her quirks—her lopsided pounce,
I give her treats, and she'll surmount.

So here's to blunders, day by day,
Life's silly moments, come what may!
In every laugh and little grin,
Gratitude dances deep within.

The Gift of Noticing

A squirrel once stole my peanut stash,
I chased him down, but he was brash.
In every nut he pockets tight,
I find a joy, my heart's delight.

The flowers bloom, but bees don't care,
They zoom around like they own the air.
In their buzzing chorus, I hear a tune,
An orchestra under the afternoon moon.

The neighbor's garden is quite the sight,
With flamingos plastic, oh what a fright!
But every glance sparks a tiny cheer,
In quirky sights, the joys appear.

So here I sit, beneath the trees,
Finding laughter in the gentle breeze.
In simple things, I see the light,
And note them down in pure delight.

Echoes of Kindness Resounding

A stranger smiled, and I felt bold,
I shared my fries, a tale retold.
In every bite, a bond was made,
With ketchup laughs that never fade.

The dog park chaos, what a show,
With pups who dart and then lay low.
Each wagging tail's a thankful shout,
In their frolics, I've no doubt.

The neighbor's music blares so loud,
Yet in the chaos, I'm quite proud.
For every beat that rattles my peace,
I shake along, let worries cease.

So here's to kindness, wild and free,
The echoes bounce, they sing to me.
In little acts we find a way,
To make the most of every day.

Cradled in Care's Embrace

Mom's cooking smells like pure delight,
Even burnt toast is a taste of light.
Her laughter bubbles, pot's a-boil,
In those moments, my worries uncoil.

Dad's dad jokes? They're quite the art,
Each punchline hits right from the heart.
In every groan and eye roll wide,
I find affection, can't help but side.

The neighbor's cat thinks he owns my chair,
But I share my seat; I don't really care.
With every purr and playful swat,
I know I've got a little love plot.

So here we sit, together we thrive,
In these little quirks, we truly arrive.
It's laughter, love, and a warm embrace,
In all these moments, I find my place.

Finding Joy in the Mundane

Waking up to coffee's smell,
Socks that magically don't smell.
A cat that trips while chasing light,
My breakfast burns, but that's alright.

The laundry's dancing, detergent's cheer,
A vacuum cleaner, oh so near.
Every chore feels like a show,
Who knew dust bunnies could steal the show?

Walking on a sidewalk bright,
Oh look, a squirrel, what a sight!
Life's little quirks, a treasure chest,
In tiny moments, we feel blessed.

So let's toast our daily grind,
For silly antics, we can find.
With laughter echoing through the air,
In this zany life, we'll always share.

The Glitter of Grateful Days

On Mondays, coffee spills, oh joy,
My old shoelaces, a funky toy.
A whimsy here, a mishap there,
Grateful giggles fill the air.

Oh, Tuesday's toast is burnt again,
I shout, then laugh, "You are my friend!"
Wednesday's socks — They never pair,
But I just dance like I don't care.

Thursday brings me a joyful mess,
As I trip over my own red dress.
Friday sings with silly tunes,
Under the glow of laughing moons.

So here's to days that make us grin,
With every blunder, let joy begin.
In the chaos, we take our stance,
And find the glitter in life's dance.

When Silence Speaks Thanks

In quiet corners of the day,
I trip on thoughts that love to play.
Silence wraps me in a hug,
As I savor that last cold mug.

When no one's here, I dance alone,
With my sock puppet as my clone.
Bumbling jokes, a one-man show,
In silence, gratitude does glow.

A whisper floats on gentle air,
Invisible thanks, I swear,
For little things that make me smile,
Like finding lost socks once in a while.

So let's embrace the quiet night,
And thank the stars for every light.
With laughter echoing in our hearts,
Even silence is full of arts.

Dance of the Thankful Heart

In the kitchen, I take the lead,
Dodging flour like I'm a steed.
A dance-off with the toaster, bright,
Crispy bread, this feels so right.

I twirl with pots and pans anew,
Ballet moves with a ladle, too.
A jig on spills, slips, and mess,
In the chaos, we're truly blessed.

Spin around, the dog joins in,
He's my partner, and I can't win.
Laughing hard while we both sway,
In every step, joy leads the way.

So let's conga with our dreams tonight,
Life's a party, and it feels so right.
With every beat of happy art,
We celebrate with a thankful heart.

The Tapestry of Thanks

In the wild world of socks and shoes,
I'm grateful for the absence of blues.
When life gives lemons, I make a pie,
And eat it quickly, oh me, oh my!

The cat that yawns like it owns the sun,
Gives me snickers, oh what fun!
With dishes piled high, I giggle and grin,
For laughter's the best way to begin.

Gifts of the Moment

Frogs in my garden make quite a show,
Croaking their hearts out, stealing the show.
I thank the toaster for crispy bread,
A morning without it? Oh, dread!

Socks full of holes, they dance on my feet,
Grateful for snacks that are sugary sweet.
Each moment's a treasure, I pause and I seize,
Even my blender does as it pleases!

Beneath the Boughs of Kindness

The neighbor brings cookies, oh what delight,
Makes me wonder, did she bake them all night?
Each grin that I share makes my heart do a leap,
While squirrels steal shiny things, oh so deep.

Beneath the old tree, we laugh and we play,
Throwing acorns like it's a fun game of tay.
With kindness like candy, life's sweet to the core,
Here's to more giggles—who could ask for more?

Thankful for the Simple Joys

For bubble wrap popping, it's pure heaven sent,
A therapy session, with every 'pop' spent.
Each mealtime's a circus, the dog steals a fry,
As I shake my head, who could ever deny?

Sunshine and rain make the garden a show,
With veggies and flowers all putting on glow.
For clouds that look like marshmallows high,
A giggle escapes, as I sigh in the sky!

A Journey of Thankful Steps

In my shoes, I skip and hop,
Grateful for the candy shop.
Each lollipop, a sweet delight,
Sugar high takes me to flight.

Bumping into friends each day,
With silly jokes, we laugh and play.
A thanks to coffee's morning cheer,
Keeps my brain from disappearing!

For sunny days and rainy nights,
For pizza parties and city lights.
Each moment shared, a treasure found,
In gratefulness, we're tightly bound.

So here's a toast with silly hats,
To all the joy, the love, the chats.
With every step, my spirits rise,
In the dance of life, hear my sighs!

The Stillness of Gratitude's Embrace

In the calm of morning's light,
I find a world that feels just right.
With socks mismatched, I sip my tea,
Thankful for a cozy spree.

The cat's soft purr, a gentle score,
And crumbs I leave on kitchen floor.
To burnt toast and jelly spills,
Life's little flops bring hearty thrills.

Each moment's like a joke well-told,
With laughter ringing, never old.
For all the fails that make me grin,
In the tapestry of life, I win.

So here's to quirks and silly paths,
To all the fun and goofy laughs.
In the stillness, blessings pour,
A giggle fit, who could ask for more?

Kindred Spirits of Thankfulness

With friends who wear the socks of glee,
We share the joys of bumblebees.
A grateful song, we hum along,
In nuts and giggles, we belong.

To pizza crusts and cheeky pranks,
To handstands done on sandy banks.
Each goofy dance, a tale to tell,
With each shared laugh, we know it well.

The silly hats and messy art,
Have painted joy upon my heart.
To all the quirks that fill our days,
We hold each other in warm rays.

So let's rejoice in friendly flames,
For wacky pairs and silly games.
Together, we create our song,
In the rhythm of where we belong.

Shimmering Reflections of Appreciation

In mirrors cracked, our smiles show,
With silly grins, they softly glow.
A thanks for friends who make it bright,
In our odd ways, we shed delight.

The puddles splash with joyful kicks,
As laughter dances, joy's sweet tricks.
For wobbly bikes and cake gone wrong,
In every stumble, we feel strong.

For winks and nudges shared at dusk,
In quiet moments, ah, the rust!
Life's little laughs, like sprinkles here,
Make ordinary days so dear.

So here's a nod to life's fine quirks,
To coffee spills and playful jerks.
In shimmering joys, we find our way,
With grateful hearts, we seize the day!

The Stillness of Appreciation

In a world that's always loud,
I find peace in the crowd.
Cheers to coffee spills and toast,
For the little things I love the most.

With socks that never match my shoes,
I laugh at my own silly views.
Thank you, oh precious laundry pile,
You make me smile in a quirky style.

Some days it feels like I'm a mess,
But hey, who doesn't like a little stress?
To each hiccup, I raise a cheer,
Grateful for laughter that's always near.

So here's to quirks, and clumsy falls,
And the joy that at least always calls.
I'll keep appreciating the fun in life,
Even if I trip over my own strife.

Petals of Positivity

Dancing daisies in the breeze,
Who knew you could bring me ease?
Thank you, clumsy bunnies too,
For hopping joyfully into view!

Oh, the blissful mess of cake,
Missing the pan? What a mistake!
But each crumb is a reason to grin,
Celebrate mishaps, let the fun begin!

Sunshine on a rainy day,
Giggles hiding in the hay.
Grateful for puddles that splash about,
Life's silly moments give me clout!

To every wobble and every tilt,
I raise my glass, "This is my guilt!"
For in this chaos, I find delight,
And bloom with laughter, oh what a sight!

An Invitation to Remember

Hey there, memory, come and play,
Let's relive the goofy ballet!
Remember all the silly pranks?
Gratitude flows like a river of thanks!

That time I wore my shirt backward,
The laughter came like a silly herd.
Let's toast to the days of spilled tea,
And fond memories that set us free!

With each awkward dance and quirky dance,
Life whispers, 'Hey, take a chance!'
So here's to every silly slip,
And the comfort of each friendship trip!

As we gather 'round this joyful table,
Let's enjoy the tales we're able.
For every giggle that we share,
Is a sprinkle of joy beyond compare!

The Heart's Gentle Nod

Oh what a day, with bananas on my head,
An unexpected style, never dread!
I thank the fruit for this bold flair,
Making even critics stop and stare!

Grateful for socks that seem to vanish,
And shoes that often have a banish.
Each lost item leads to a chuckle,
Finding treasures in every shuffle.

With silly faces and wobble-grins,
I thank the universe for the spins.
Each stumble teaches me to dance,
See the humor in every chance!

So here's to laughter, here's to joy,
From every girl and every boy.
Celebrating life with a soft little laugh,
In the wackiness, I find my path!

A Symphony of Thankful Thoughts

In the morning, coffee brews,
I dance like I can't lose.
A toast to socks without holes,
Cheers to life and all its roles.

Thankful for the cat's weird stare,
For neighbor's funny purple hair.
Gratitude for jelly beans,
And those chaotic kitchen scenes.

For awkward laughs and silly pranks,
Singing songs, we raise our flanks.
A nod to socks that don't quite match,
Or friends who love a good free snatch.

So here's to life, a wobbly ride,
With grateful hearts we glide and slide.
In this symphony of small joys,
Life's a trip, let's be the toys.

The Colors of Contentment

An orange slice upon my plate,
Turns my frown into a mate.
Blue jeans with a coffee stain,
Still, I dance in the pouring rain.

Thankful for that purple hat,
And every unexpected spat.
A rainbow creeps through all the fuss,
Life's a canvas, paint for us.

A splash of pink on Mondays gray,
Like swings that spin you all the way.
Yellows burst from every smile,
Let's gratitude go wild for a while.

So let's wear shades of laughter bright,
In silly games of sheer delight.
Colors swirl, let worries fade,
Life's a joke, a grand parade.

Thankful Ripples in Time

With each splash a giggle glows,
Ripples dance, and silly flows.
Thankful for the ice cream melt,
And all the joy that summer dealt.

A leap for joy on muddy grass,
A quick trip, watch the grown-ups pass.
Thankful for the noise and cheer,
And all those moments we hold dear.

A wobbly bike upon the street,
Pedaling laughter with happy feet.
Each trip, a stumble mixed with glee,
Life's a circus, come join me.

In ripples vast, we play and glide,
With gratitude, we laugh and ride.
Every splash a memory made,
Echoes of joy that never fade.

Moments Wrapped in Gratitude

In fuzzy socks on winter nights,
Thankful giggles, silly flights.
Moments wrapped in hugs so tight,
Like marshmallows in hot cocoa's bite.

A card game where we're far too loud,
On the couch, we feel so proud.
Thankful for our silly memes,
And all the wacky, wild dreams.

Jokes that land with a funny thud,
A leap into a snowy puddle's flood.
Grateful for the friends who tease,
Life's a riddle, done with ease.

So round we go, a thankful spin,
With laughter, grins, and joyful din.
Wrapped in moments ripe and sweet,
Life's a puzzle, a treat to meet.

Anthems of Acknowledgment

In the fridge, my snack lies bold,
A treasure trove, worth more than gold.
I nod to the maker, a chef so grand,
For peanut butter, I'll give a hand.

The dog fetched the ball, with great delight,
He's my MVP, my furry knight.
His wagging tail, a joyful cheer,
For fetching my shoe, he's now a dear.

The rain comes down with a big splash,
I see puddles and jump in with a dash.
Thank you, clouds, for this watery fun,
Who needs a pool when you're on the run?

And when I trip on that same old mat,
I laugh it off like a jovial cat.
Cheers to the world for the little falls,
Where giggles rise and gratitude calls.

The Quietude of Gratitude

Coffee brews like a morning song,
Its scent envelops, where I belong.
Thanks to the beans, rich and bold,
For keeping my mornings, fun and told.

The cat on the windowsill rests so fine,
She stretches her paws, says, 'This sun is mine!'
In her lazy snooze, peace reigns supreme,
A soft reminder of life's cozy theme.

When socks go missing, and shoes don't match,
I chuckle at fate, such a funny patch.
Thanks for the chaos, the playful twist,
Without these mishaps, what would I miss?

A chuckle from friends at my silly jokes,
Each laugh worth more than all the hoax.
In this circus of life, I find my phase,
With every smile, I count the ways.

Wings of Graceful Acceptance

Like a butterfly flapping on a breezy day,
I greet the world in my quirky way.
Thank you, dear life, for your laughable quirks,
For each little slip, and all of my perks.

In the kitchen, I drop a spoon or two,
Making a mess, oh, who knew?
With flour on my face, I strike a pose,
Thank you, mishaps, for the fun you impose.

A friend called me up, sharing some news,
He's finally bought a pair of blue shoes.
I shout, 'Well done!' as cups start to clang,
In life's little wins, we all can hang.

As the clock strikes twelve, I might feel snacky,
Those late-night cravings, oh, so wacky.
Gratitude for chips, and ice cream galore,
For these tasty treats, I'll forever implore.

A Cascade of Thankful Moments

Raindrops dance on the window pane,
Each one a reminder, I've got no pain.
Thanks, umbrellas, for flipping inside out,
What a sight you make, no room for doubt.

The cat's in a box, her throne of dreams,
Watching the world with her catnip schemes.
Thanks for the silly, the purr and the meow,
For laughter that sprouts from my heart, here and now.

My friend tried to cook, what a delight!
The smoke alarm chimed, but spirits were bright.
Thank you, kitchen, for your chaos and woes,
In the best of scenes, a friendship grows.

And when laughter echoes late into the night,
In the glow of our giggles, everything feels right.
For every moment wrapped in hilarious whim,
I raise my glass to the joys that brim.

Rejoicing in the Little Things

I woke up to coffee, oh what a treat!
The aroma around me, can't be beat.
My toast danced with jelly, a sticky embrace,
And my socks, mismatched, still won the race.

The cat on the windowsill, a royal decree,
Chasing shadows like it's a big jamboree.
The sun tickles my nose, making me grin,
Thankful for the laughs; let the fun begin!

A shoe with a hole, what a funny sight,
Yet it carried my dreams to a wondrous height.
Each tiny moment, like confetti in air,
Life's quirks and its giggles, oh, how they flare!

So here's to the small things, a whimsical toast,
For slip-ups and hiccups, I cherish the most.
In a world that can tumble, I'll hold my ground,
With joy in my heart, it's laughter I've found.

A Wish for Thankfulness

A wish for the silly, let's giggle today,
Like socks in the dryer, that ran off to play.
I'm grateful for hiccups, they make me feel free,
Especially the ones that come out with a "pee!"

The traffic light dances, then turns lovely green,
While I sing in my car like I'm on a queen's screen.
A sandwich that slips, what a daring delight,
With mustard on my face, I still feel so bright!

My dog with a grin, he's a furry old clown,
Rolling 'round in the grass, where's my sad frown?
The world's got its quirks, oh, how they do shine,
I'll toast with my juice, and say, "Life is just fine!"

So here's a cheer, for laughter and jest,
I'm thankful, dear universe, you're simply the best!
For each giggle and snort, I'll raise up my glass,
With a wink and a grin, let the fun never pass.

In Bloom: Harvesting Gratitude

Gardens of giggles, in colors they bloom,
With daisies that tickle, they lighten the gloom.
I planted my sneakers, a curious sight,
And danced 'round the sprout with sheer delight!

The squirrels act like jesters, bold acrobats,
Stealing my snacks; hey! Give them back, brats!
Yet I can't help but chuckle, they're quick on their toes,
Grateful for their chaos, and the laughter it shows.

Sunshine is winking, the clouds play along,
Whistling a tune like a jukebox in song.
With laughter like raindrops, falling so fast,
Each moment a treasure, forever to last.

So here's to the blooms, both silly and bright,
Harvesting moments that dance in the light.
In fields of our laughter, let our spirits soar,
With hearts full of humor, let's open the door!

A Journey in Acknowledgment

Off on a journey, my map upside down,
Lost in my thoughts, but still wearing a crown.
With snacks in my pocket, I venture anew,
And wave to the llamas, what more can I do?

The roads twist and turn, just like my hair,
Each bump in the road leads to laughter to share.
I trip on my shoelace, and into a bush,
Thank goodness for nature, it gives me a push!

The signs all say "Caution," but what does that mean?
Is it laughter that spills from a screen on a screen?
The sun's shining bright, or is it my glow?
Thankful for the memories, where I fall and I grow.

So here's to this journey, each stumble and fall,
To the joy that it brings, let's continue this call.
With gratitude blooming, like flowers in spring,
I'll dance down this path, let the laughter take wing!

Blossoms of Thankfulness

In a garden where gratitude blooms,
The flowers giggle, dispelling gloom.
We water them with quirky jokes,
And dance around like silly folks.

The sun shines bright, they sway and prance,
Thanks to the pot that's got no chance.
With farts and giggles, we celebrate,
Growing joy up high, oh isn't it great?

Bumblebees buzz with quite the flair,
They tickle petals, dance in the air.
Each bloom a chuckle, a homage pure,
To all that's silly, and joy that's sure.

So here's to laughter, each chuckle a wave,
Through roots of mischief, we merrily rave.
Let blossoms of gladness forever provide,
A patch for our smiles, a silly joyride.

A Dance of Joyful Acknowledgment

With two left feet, we take a chance,
And trip through life in a goofy dance.
Each twirl a nod to the quirks we love,
Thankfulness bubbling, like laughs from above.

We wave our arms like windmill sails,
While friends laugh loud, they catch their fails.
Thank you, oh banana peels we found,
For making our antics so fun and sound.

In shoes untied, we leap and bound,
A quirk-filled waltz, joy unbound.
We thank the floor for all its slips,
A merry ride on our laughter trips.

So join the party, come take a spin,
With every misstep, we all go in.
Our clumsy moves, a joyful delight,
A dance of thanks, oh what a sight!

Reflection in the Pool of Thanks

At the pond where ducks float happily,
We splash around like it's a spree.
Each ripple echoes, oinking glee,
Thank you, dear ducks, for your quacky spree.

I see my face in the water's dance,
With sips of wisdom, it's quite the romance.
The frogs croak back with a wisecrack,
Thank you, dear friends, for the laughter stack.

As lilies bloom with their goofy grace,
We giggle at frogs with their ribbiting pace.
Each splosh of joy is a message here,
To cherish the fun, oh crystal clear!

So come take a dip in this pond of cheer,
Where laughter gets loud, and worries disappear.
With every splash, our hearts seem to grow,
In the pool of giggles, let gratitude flow.

The Beauty of Recognizing

Oh, what a sight when messes collide,
With spaghetti hats, we take rib-tickling pride.
For every mishap, we smirk and wink,
Thank you, dear bloopers, for making us think!

Like ketchup spills and mustard sneezes,
Our gratitude rises like autumn leaves.
A tumble here, a pratfall there,
Life's silly moments, we joyfully share.

In jumbled words, we offer our thanks,
To blunders that fill our endless pranks.
Recognizing chaos with a cackle loud,
We thank the blunders, good times unbowed.

So raise your glass to the humor divine,
In each little quirk, there's a straight-up line.
With beauty in folly, our hearts may dance,
A celebration of life, in every chance!

Lanterns of Appreciation

Oh dear potato, you make me laugh,
For mashed or fried, you're my better half.
When you roll on by, I can't help but cheer,
For every crispy bite brings you so near.

Thank you, great coffee, for waking me up,
Your daily jolt fills my grateful cup.
Without your strong magic, I'd hit the hay,
Snoring away while the world starts to play.

High fives to my socks, you keep me warm,
With stripes and polka dots, you bring the charm.
In mismatched glory, you dance in my drawer,
Each time I wear you, I can't help but roar.

Cheers to my plants, you're my leafy pals,
You breathe out good vibes, no need for scowls.
When I forget to water, you still stand tall,
Reminding me gently, "You feed us all!"

Where Gratitude Blooms

Oh silly broccoli, you make me smile,
With your verdant head, you're worth my while.
In salads and stir-fries, you always shine,
Thank you for roughing it on my divine line.

To my old guitar, I strum and sing loud,
You make me feel like I'm part of the crowd.
With each pluck and strum, I feel so alive,
In the rhythm of thanks, together we thrive.

Call out to chocolate, so sweet and neat,
You turn frowns upside down, a glorious treat.
With every square broken, a smile appears,
Your gooey goodness wipes away my fears.

Here's to my cat, who's a fluffy diva,
Mysterious and sly, makes me a believer.
With each little purr as you steal my chair,
I thank you for moments that we two share.

In the Quiet of Thankfulness

Oh what joy my cereal brings to the morn,
With milk or with yogurt, it calms the storm.
You snap, crackle, and pop, a lively cheer,
Each spoonful I take, I'm thankful, oh dear!

To my trusty old jacket, you keep me warm,
In rain or in shine, you're my fashion charm.
When the wind blows hard, you hug me tight,
A shield against chill, my cozy delight.

Grateful for sunsets that paint the sky bright,
With hues that dance gently, oh what a sight!
Each evening brings magic with colors that bloom,
A canvas of thanks, dispelling the gloom.

Thanks to my neighbors, always so loud,
With music and laughter, they form a crowd.
They keep life exciting, with antics that play,
In this little theatre, we cheers every day.

Threads of Gratitude Weaving Us Together

Oh socks from the dryer, where do you hide?
I thank you for laughter, my mismatched pride.
Each morning's adventure, a puzzle to solve,
With these funky steps, our joys evolve.

Here's to the mugs, each one has a tale,
Some chipped with love, others on sale.
With every hot sip that warms my soul,
You offer a moment where calm takes its toll.

Thanks to my shoes, though you squeak and groan,
You walk alongside me, I'm never alone.
Together we wander through puddles and parks,
In journeys of thanks that ignite joyful sparks.

A nod to the games, that we play and fight,
In laughter and silliness, you bring pure light.
Each roll of the dice, an adventure anew,
In threads of our joy, I'm woven to you.

Gratitude's Quiet Power

In the morning, I cheer my toast,
Butter on a bagel, I love it the most.
Thankful for donuts, oh what a treat,
Calories don't count, when joy is sweet.

A parking spot close to the door,
Feels like winning the gratitude score.
When the coffee's strong and pants still fit,
I smile and think, 'I'm quite the hit!'

A cat that purrs, a dog that wags,
Little things tally like gratitude tags.
Each silly moment, a gem to collect,
I giggle through life, what else to expect?

So raise your cup and let's give a cheer,
For laughter and love that bring us near.
Life's shining gems, they sparkle and dance,
In the silliness, we find our chance.

A Mosaic of Abundant Joy

With sprinkles on cupcakes, I feel so bright,
A rainbow of flavor, pure delight.
Each bite is a laugh, a sugary grin,
Why stop at one? Let the fun begin!

The neighbor's cat thinks it owns my yard,
While I chase it off, my demeanor's marred.
But as it sprawls out, all fluffy and fat,
I can't help but giggle at that silly brat.

The socks that never match, a life in style,
A fashion choice that makes you smile.
In chaos and mess, gratitude shines,
For the quirks of this life are truly divine!

So here's to the chaos, the blissfully loud,
The moments that leave us grinning proud.
In every absurdity, joy's always there,
A mosaic of laughter, a love we share.

Kindness in Every Breath

A sneeze on the bus, oh what a scene,
Everyone looks, like I'm so obscene.
But laughter erupts, kindness takes flight,
A shared chuckle bonds us, oh what a sight!

The old man who smiles, as he walks his dog,
The way he waves, a true heartthrob.
In every small gesture, each silly grin,
Kindness is vengeance, let the fun begin!

When life gives you lemons, make lemon pie,
Or find some friends to share your sly.
With jokes in our pockets, we'll dance and sing,
For joy is a treasure, the simplest thing.

So breathe in the kindness, let giggles unfurl,
In this wacky world, give chaos a whirl.
With each hearty laugh and snicker we share,
Life blooms like flowers, fragrant and rare.

Thankful Whispers in the Wind

The wind carries whispers, oh so sly,
Telling me thanks as the leaves fly by.
Every rustle and giggle, a note of delight,
While squirrels plot mischief, oh what a sight!

Thankful for hiccups and on-the-spot jokes,
For puns that can turn all of us into folks.
In the shuffle of life and its quirky bends,
Find joy in odd moments, they're the best friends.

The sun on my face, a warm fuzzy hug,
Comfy and cozy like a big, furry bug.
In quirky connections, we gather our knits,
A tapestry woven in smiles and fits.

So here's to the whispers upon the breeze,
To laughter and joy that always appease.
With gratitude echoed, in hearts we'll mend,
May the funny moments never truly end.

Embracing the Gift of Now

The toast is burnt, but hey, who cares?
Laughing with crumbs, we dance in pairs.
A sock is missing, its match forlorn,
Yet here we are, together reborn.

The coffee's cold, like my morning cheer,
But hugs and giggles bring warmth near.
We stumble and trip on life's silly stage,
Yet each blunder turns a new page.

The time is now, let's make it bright,
With silly faces and pure delight.
A gift of laughter, wrapped in gold,
A treasure trove of stories told.

In this mad dance, our spirits soar,
Hand in hand, let's revel some more.
In chaos and joy, we find our way,
Collecting moments, come what may.

The Language of Appreciation

Your jeans are stained, what did you eat?
But your silly grin is my favorite treat.
Thanks for the laughter, and all your quirks,
In the language of joy, let's trade our perks.

We spill our drinks, we spill our tea,
Yet every oops brings more glee to see.
From pun-filled jests to inside jokes,
We giggle loud, and roll like blokes.

Missing socks and tattered shoes,
Still, in this life, we simply choose.
To giggle, grin, and sing our tunes,
In every silence, gratitude blooms.

A toast to us - the silly, the fun!
Joy really shines when days are done.
With all our flaws, we shine so bright,
In the spectrum of love, we ignite!

In the Arms of Serenity

In quiet moments, where the chaos dims,
We find our peace in jumbled whims.
A cat on the keyboard, a dog with a hat,
Serenity swirls in the chaos of that.

The laundry's piled, a mountain for sure,
But each little mess opens the door.
To laughter that fills the stillest of nights,
In the arms of calm, everything's right.

Coffee spills, and the world just shakes,
But joy is found in the choice that makes.
To spin in circles, waltzing with fate,
Filled with the mirth that we celebrate.

Embracing the quirks, in every embrace,
Finding our joy in this lovely space.
With laughter as armor, we dance on our toes,
In a world bursting sweet, thanks overflow.

Gratitude's Sweet Serenade

When life throws lemons, we juggle and laugh,
Squeezing joy, finding our path.
With every mishap, we tune our song,
In this duet, we fiercely belong.

A car that won't start, but who cares, right?
We'll laugh 'til dawn, we'll light up the night.
In moments of chaos, we find our way,
With humor blooming, come what may.

Bumps and bruises, we take in stride,
Finding the fun in this crazy ride.
Through trials and giggles, we string each note,
A serenade sung as we all stroke.

So here's to the days, both wild and sweet,
Where love grows louder in every heartbeat.
Amidst the laughter, our hearts expand wide,
In gratitude's glow, let's take this ride!

A Garden Rich in Gratitude

In the garden where weeds grow,
I chuckle at things I now know.
The daisies dance, a wild parade,
Thank you, plants, for the shade!

The tomatoes blush with glee,
With every bite, they shout, "Whee!"
I trip over tools with a grin,
Grateful even when I spin!

Beet and carrot sing a tune,
Proudly waving 'neath the moon.
In this patch of joy, I dwell,
Thank you, veggies, you're swell!

With every sprout and every bloom,
I dance around with little room.
In gratitude, my laughter rings,
Life's a garden full of things!

The Art of Thanking Life.

Thank you for the socks that clash,
The cupboards that make me dash.
For coffee spills that stain my shirt,
And the days when I trip in the dirt!

The cat that meows at the wrong hour,
Turns me into a morning flower.
For burnt toast that tastes like a brick,
I'll laugh it off with a quick flick!

Thank you for the neighbor's dog,
Who thinks my yard's a big ol' bog.
For every odd and quirky thing,
Life's a joy when you let it swing!

With every wobble, every misstep,
I giggle and take another prep.
Such a ride full of silly strife,
Oh, the art of thanking life!

Gratitude's Gentle Whisper

In the kitchen, a dance of pots,
Making meals, forgetting thoughts.
Thank you for the smoke that rolls,
And the pizza that takes its toll!

Thank you for the socks that roam,
Finding them feels like coming home.
In the laundry, a strange surprise,
An oddball sock, in all its size!

The shower's song, a steady beat,
Grateful for those chlorine feet.
With soap bubbles in my hair,
I'm thankful, though it's quite a scare!

Each little laugh, each tiny cheer,
Gratitude whispers loud and clear.
In the mess, I find my bliss,
A simple joy I can't dismiss!

Bowing to the Beauty of Gratitude

With a bow to my overflowing sink,
I wonder why they all seem to blink.
Thank you, dishes, for this grand show,
You make me dance, my own tableau!

To the socks that dance without their mate,
A fashion choice that's worth the wait.
For every item that goes astray,
I'm grateful for my scenic play!

The coffee mug that's always chipped,
With it, my worries are equipped.
Thank you for the mornings late,
Each delay feels like a fate!

Bowing low to this joyful fuss,
I find my giggles in the bus.
In chaos, there's a loving plea,
For all the things that make me, me!

The Harvest of Appreciation

In the garden of gratitude, I sow,
With seeds of laughter, they grow.
I trip on joy, fall in delight,
These moments make everything right.

Potatoes of kindness, carrots of cheer,
I gather them all, a fine harvest here.
Tomatoes plump with unforgettable fun,
Who knew thanks could weigh a ton?

Pumpkins of laughter, squash with glee,
Each veggie sings, 'You're great, can't you see?'
The more I gather, the sillier I feel,
This crop of mirth is the real deal!

At the feast of joy, I serve it all,
With a side of giggles, we have a ball.
If you can't find me, I'm holed up in bliss,
Thanking the universe with a hearty laugh and a kiss!

Echoes of Thankfulness

In the hall of echoes, it's loud and clear,
Gratitude dances, give a cheer!
The claps of joy bounce off the walls,
As thankfulness tiptoes, giggling in the halls.

I hear 'thank you' in the toilet's flush,
A laughter-filled rush in a silly hush.
Each echoing giggle, round and wild,
It's thankfulness, behaving like a child.

Bouncing off walls with playful grace,
Thanks and chuckles spin around the place.
With every shout, I can't help but grin,
For gratitude's echo is where the fun begins!

So let's celebrate, sing loud and proud,
With a comedic twist, draw in the crowd.
These echoes of joy are my favorite sound,
In the circus of life, it's where love is found!

Sunlight on the Soul

A beam of sunshine, what a delight,
It tickles my nose, makes everything bright.
With rays of giggles dancing on my face,
I'm basking in warmth, in this joyful space.

Sunbeams laughing, it feels like a joke,
As they tag-team my mind, it's a happy poke.
Each ray a friend, with sparkling wink,
Making me stop and happily think.

I tip my hat to this luminous glow,
For gratitude's warmth makes my spirit flow.
Sunlight on my soul, it's truly divine,
Let's toast to the rays that taste like wine!

So here's to the sun, and its playful spark,
Bringing blissful moments, lighting the dark.
In this bright dance, I find my role,
With every chuckle, a sunnier soul!

A Tapestry of Grateful Moments

Stitching together moments of fun,
I weave joy into the fabric of sun.
Each laugh and giggle, a thread so bright,
Making a tapestry of sheer delight.

With patches of love and spots of cheer,
I hang them up for all to hear.
"Thank you!" whispers the yarn with glee,
In this goofy quilt, there's always a spree.

I tangled my stitches, oh what a sight,
But each knot just adds to the joy and light.
With mismatched colors and laughter entwined,
It's perfect chaos, wonderfully designed.

So let's gather 'round this colorful patch,
With memories to cherish, and a warmth to catch.
In this quilt of thanks, let's dance and play,
For life's silly moments are here to stay!

Harvest of Gratitude

In the garden of my days, we sow joy,
Each laugh like a seed, oh boy oh boy!
With every meal shared, each clumsy dance,
We harvest the moments, not leaving to chance.

The cat steals my sandwich, I'm starting to think,
Reality's funny, I give him a wink.
With family around, the jokes come alive,
In this quirky harvest, we always survive.

When life hands a lemon, I make lemonade,
With extra giggles, a fine charade.
Counting our blessings, adding some spice,
Gratitude blooms, oh it's so nice!

At the end of the day, we sit and we cheer,
For all of these moments, I hold so dear.
Though life's not perfect, it surely does spark,
In this harvest of joy, we leave our mark.

Rays of Thankfulness

Morning sun tickles, right on my nose,
With coffee in hand, I strike a silly pose.
Thank you, dear coffee, for each caffeine hit,
You brighten my day and make it legit.

The toast pops up, a breakfast delight,
Burnt edges and laughter, what a funny sight!
I'd thank the toaster, but it's broken too,
A gratitude moment, oh what will I do?

With friends by my side, we're a wacky crew,
Telling tall tales, just like we do.
Each story a treasure, on this joy ride,
With rays of laughter, we're swelling with pride.

As evening falls, a dance break so sweet,
We twirl and we sway, tapping our feet.
Thanks to the music, and laughs that we share,
In these rays of joy, life's burdens are rare.

The Canvas of Thankful Moments

On a canvas of life, I splash with bright hues,
With colors of laughter, I chase away blues.
Each stroke a giggle, each shade a delight,
In this art of thanks, everything feels right.

The messy palette of my daily grind,
Is filled with the quirks of a jolly mind.
Paint spills and oops, it's part of the game,
In this wild masterpiece, it's never the same.

With friends as my muses, we laugh until cried,
We sketch out the moments, side by side.
Each funny fail, a stroke on the page,
In this gallery of life, we're all center stage.

At the end of the day, we look at our work,
With smiles at the canvas, we never smirk.
For every wild splash, a memory made,
In this joyous art, gratitude's displayed.

Reflections in a Thankful Mind

In mirror reflections, what do I see?
A bunch of odd moments, full of glee.
With hair that's a mess and a grin ear to ear,
I thank all my mishaps, they bring me good cheer.

When shoes go mismatched, I just give a laugh,
Thankful for chaos, it's my better half.
Each stumble and trip, a dance of delight,
In this clumsy world, I'm feeling so right.

The mirror keeps cracking, oh what a joke!
With every new chip, I start feeling woke.
So cheers to the laughter, the joy and the fun,
In this quirky reflection, we shine like the sun.

So here's to the moments that make my heart sing,
In laughter and chaos, we find the sweet spring.
With open minds, we embrace every turn,
In life's funny mirror, there's so much to learn.

A Melody of Cautionary Thanks

I'm grateful for the socks, they never match,
But on my feet, they help me as I dash.
And thankful for the mornings, though I yawn,
Their bitter coffee helps me keep on, drawn.

Oh, thanks for all the fruits gone slightly bad,
Your squishy apple made me very sad.
Yet in the mess, a lesson shines so bright,
Next time, I'll just check the fridge each night.

For every time my keys go missing fast,
I thank the floor for hiding treasures past.
Without this quest of searching high and low,
I'd never learn how to abstractly grow.

So here's to all the mishaps in my day,
I take a bow, and then I dance away.
With laughter in the air, I raise a toast,
To all the things I thank, and I can boast.

Serenading the Moments

I'm thankful for the dust that can't be swept,
It settles in my mind where thoughts have crept.
And gratitude for neighbors loud at night,
Their karaoke brings a certain fright.

Oh, how I cherish all those lost remotes,
They teach me patience, as my brain just gloats.
For every burned-up dinner I've cooked right,
I'm grateful for the takeout that feels light.

Each crack in the pavement, a story told,
Of sneakers tripping, cozily uncontrolled.
And thankful for the times I trip and fall,
They heel my pride, making me stand tall.

So here's the song, in laughter it is singed,
With joyful thanks, my gratitude's unhinged.
In every goof-up, there's magic, I find,
A symphony of joys—delightfully unrefined.

The Luminescence of Gratitude

Thanks for my plants, they're just so alive,
Though I swear they plot how to survive.
Grateful for the bread that often lays stale,
Each slice a reminder that I can't fail.

Oh, the joy of laundry, it's such a jest,
Finding all those socks that just will not rest.
And thanks for every splatter in the kitchen,
Culinary art with a little glitch in.

For blunders in my texting, oh what a thrill,
That autocorrect gives my friends a chill.
Each slip a blessing, with humor in each fright,
Making random moments feel just so right.

So let's raise a toast, to mishaps galore,
For every laugh shared, I can't help but roar.
In all the chaos, there's light to be found,
A grateful heart, in giggles, is unbound.

Reflections on a Grateful Day

Thanks for the sunshine that plays hide and seek,
It's like a game, very silly, not weak.
I'm grateful for puddles and shoes that squish,
Each splash a reminder of childhood's wish.

Oh, my morning hair—a glorious fright,
A crown of chaos, such a comical sight.
And thanks to my cat, who thinks he's a king,
His royal demands make my heart take wing.

For every meeting that could have been an email,
I smile and nod, it's part of the deal.
Each awkward silence, a chance to unwind,
Its humor wrapped tight, like a student's mind.

So here's to the laughter I find every day,
In odd little places, it's here to stay.
With a wink and a nod, I gladly confess,
This life full of quirks is simply the best!

Gratitude's Whisper

With socks that match, I'm feeling bright,
Thankful for mishaps that feel just right.
My coffee's strong, my pants are tight,
　Each little joy brings pure delight.

I tripped on air, oh what a scene,
Grateful for laughter, you know what I mean.
A cat that snores, a friend that's keen,
　Life's silly moments in between.

The fridge is bare, yet I still feast,
On pizza crusts, I'm quite the beast.
My rubber chicken brings me peace,
In a world of chaos, it's my favorite piece.

So here's my cheer for the quirks of fate,
For shoes that squeak and food that's late.
In every blunder, there's love innate,
　And every giggle's worth the wait.

Seasons of A Grateful Soul

Spring brings flowers that bloom with glee,
While bees buzz loudly, just like me.
I thank the sun for my tan's decree,
And winter's chill for my hot cup of tea.

Summer days are best with fries,
Grateful for sunshine and seagull cries.
Ice cream drips, oh what a surprise—
Sticky fingers, but how time flies!

Autumn's leaves dance, quite the show,
I trip on pumpkins, but go with the flow.
Thankful for sweaters; warm hugs, you know?
Each fall brings laughter, goofiness in tow.

Winter's cold, but hot cocoa's near,
Grateful for cookies baked with cheer.
Slippers so fuzzy, I hold them dear,
In every season, joy's always here.

Echoes of Appreciation

I shout thanks to the toaster, my morning mate,
For perfect golden bread that seals my fate.
Though it pops too loud, I celebrate,
Its crispy gift always feels first-rate.

The dog that snoozes, a snorer divine,
Grateful for those wet kisses, just fine.
When muddy paws leave a trail on my wine,
I laugh as I clean, oh what a design!

For every mistake, I give a cheer,
Like burning the toast while cooking a smear.
I ride the waves of blunders so clear,
Each hiccup's a treasure, oh how sincere!

With friends who can't dance yet still try,
Grateful for chuckles that fill the sky.
Laughter's my treasure; it lifts me high,
In this raucous journey, we'll never say bye!

Blooms of Thanksgiving

I planted a garden of thankful sprout,
With all my weeds, there's no doubt.
Grateful for sunshine, without a doubt,
And pesky bugs that buzz about.

Each flower's a blunder, just like this rhyme,
Petunias that wilt make me feel sublime.
I giggle at squirrels that steal my thyme,
Grateful for nature's wild paradigm.

Dinner time's chaos, a feast in sight,
With gravy spills that feel just right.
My mashed potatoes, a sculptor's delight,
All the laughter sparkles like starlight.

So here's to the mess, the fun, and the cheer,
Grateful for moments we hold so dear.
Life's wild dance, let's give a big cheer,
For the blooms of joy that always appear.

Cherished Threads of Life

In the quilt of my days, a patch goes awry,
Missing socks and lost keys, oh my!
But laughter weaves tight, with joy that we find,
Stitching up moments, one silly line at a time.

Falling up stairs just to trip on my toes,
Yet here comes the chuckle, as my balance goes.
With every odd stumble, a smile takes flight,
A dance of appreciation, oh what a sight!

Burnt toast on mornings, a breakfast delight,
Caffeinated giggles make everything right.
Each fumble a treasure, I wouldn't exchange,
For messes and laughter, life's wonderful strange.

So raise up your mugs, cheers to the quirks,
For life's little hiccups are where the fun lurks.
With every misstep, a memory to share,
In the fabric of living, we're sewn with care.

Gratitude's Warm Embrace

Woke up this morning, the coffee was cold,
But I smiled at my mug, 'You're a sight to behold!'
With pancakes like bricks, and syrup like glue,
I chuckle out loud, it's just how I do.

Then tripped on that rug, did a little ballet,
My dog gave me side-eye, like 'Not again, eh?'
Yet with every tumble, I find funny charms,
Every little mishap wraps me in warm arms.

The neighbor's loud music, a symphony strange,
I dance to their beat, life's funny exchange.
A grateful heart giggles amidst all the din,
For in the wild chaos is where we begin.

So here's to the moments that leave us in stitches,
And to life's silly twists, that grant us our riches.
Every mischief we face, let it lift us instead,
For laughter is golden, with joy being fed!

The Heartbeat of Contentment

I opened a drawer, what a sight to behold,
A thousand old receipts, stories untold.
Each ticket a memory of where I have been,
Life's funny ongoing, a topsy-turvy spin.

Then came my old cat, with a leap and a pounce,
On the very same table, he chose to denounce.
His weighty opinion is filed with such pride,
In the court of my kitchen, he's royalty, wide.

Found joy in the chaos, a sock on the floor,
Reminds me of battles, laundry galore.
Every wrinkle, each fold, tells a tale that we find,
In this curious dance, I leave worry behind.

So here's to the laughter, the quirks we embrace,
With mishaps and mayhem, we find our own grace.
Life's sweetest rewards seem silly at first,
Fill your cup up, oh friend, let joy burst!

The Poetry of Thankful Living

In a world full of noise, there's humor to seek,
Like missing my bus, oh what a technique!
Yet I wave at the driver, a smile on my face,
'See you next week', in this silly rat race!

A mix-up at dinner, my order's gone wrong,
But I laugh it all off, it won't be long.
With friends gathered 'round, and laughter we serve,
In the blender of life, we find that sweet curve.

Each stutter and trip makes the story retold,
In the annals of friendship, where laughter unfolds.
So here's to the follies and giggles we share,
A light-hearted journey, we venture with flair.

So raise up your voices, let gratitude sing,
With jest in our hearts, oh the joy that it brings!
For every misstep is a diamond in disguise,
In this silly old life, it's the truth we reprise.

Sunlight through Grateful Eyes

Oh sunlight beams, so bright and bold,
They warm my face, like stories of old.
Thanks to the sky, for the azure play,
And clouds that drift slightly out of my way.

With each little bug that buzzes around,
I thank the ants marching under the ground.
For every mishap that brings me a grin,
Like a misplaced shoe when I'm ready to win.

Rain has its charms, it cleans the whole earth,
Just like my messy hair, such a rebirth.
So here's to the storms that make puddles gleam,
I splash and I laugh, living my dream!

Oh dear old cat, who steals my seat,
Thank you for naps and the rhythm of feet.
Life's little blessings, they tickle my soul,
With each giggle and chuckle, I'm quite the whole bowl.

A Symphony of Thankful Souls

In the choir of life, I hear a tune,
Every silly moment makes my heart swoon.
I thank the loud fridge that hums its way,
For guarding my snacks at the end of the day.

Oh socks that mismatch, what a fine disgrace,
They dance every morning, in a mismatched race.
With every lost shoe, I give a cheer,
For keeping things lively, I'm full of good cheer!

My neighbors, they chatter, with laughter so bright,
Thank you for making my evenings a delight.
For grilling in the sun, and the potluck spread,
Each dish tells a story, that keeps me well-fed.

So here's to life's quirks, like a sneeze in a crowd,
To everyone laughing, oh isn't it loud?
For the moments of joy, that keep me afloat,
I'm sailing on praise, like a very fine boat.

Whispers in the Breeze of Thanks

The wind it whispers, 'You're doing just fine,'
Thanks to the trees, when they dance on a line.
They rustle with laughter, and wiggle with glee,
"Don't take life too serious; let's have some tea!"

The bees they are buzzing, oh what a scene,
Thankful for honey, and friends who are keen.
With every small flower that pops in my view,
I chuckle and smile, oh isn't life true?

The squirrels are sneaky, they play peek-a-boo,
"Thanks for the laughter; my heart feels brand new."
With each little nut, they bury with pride,
I giggle at their antics, it's fun to abide.

So here's to the moments that make me feel great,
Thank you, sweet world, for this funny fate.
I'll dance in the breeze, with joy on my face,
With whispers of laughter, and endless embrace.

The Heart's Gentle Acknowledgment

Thank you, dear coffee, for morning's embrace,
In each frothy swirl, I find my right place.
With every spilled drop on the floor that I see,
I laugh, and I say, "Oh, that's just so me!"

Those socks in the dryer, they vanish like dreams,
I'm grateful for mysteries, or so it seems.
Each missing shoe tells a tale of its own,
But I chuckle and smile in my cozy home.

Oh pasta that twirls, in my bowl full of cheer,
Thank you for filling my belly each year.
With garlic and sauce, oh sweet delight,
I twirl on the dance floor, a chef in the night!

Here's to my gadgets that beep and that whirr,
They fill my days up like a busy old blur.
With every odd hiccup, I tip my hat high,
Here's to life's odd moments, oh me, oh my!